S0-EDJ-570

INVESTIGATING SCIENCE

Insects & Spiders

Preschool–Kindergarten

Table of Contents

www.themailbox.com

©2003 by THE EDUCATION CENTER, INC.
All rights reserved.
ISBN #1-56234-571-0

Manufactured in the United States

10 9 8 7 6 5 4 3 2 1

Insects & Spiders

Managing Editor: Allison E. Ward
Editor at Large: Diane Badden
Staff Editors: Kimberly A. Brugger, Kelly Coder
Contributing Writers: Beth Allison, Lori Alisa Burrows, Susan DeRiso, Heather Lynn Miller
Copy Editors: Tazmen Carlisle, Amy Kirtley-Hill, Karen L. Mayworth, Kristy Parton, Debbie Shoffner, Cathy Edwards Simrell
Cover Artist: Clint Moore
Art Coordinator: Greg D. Rieves
Artists: Pam Crane, Theresa Lewis Goode, Clevell Harris, Ivy L. Koonce, Sheila Krill, Clint Moore, Greg D. Rieves, Rebecca Saunders, Barry Slate, Donna K. Teal

The Mailbox® Books.com: Jennifer Tipton Bennett (DESIGNER/ARTIST); Stuart Smith (PRODUCTION ARTIST); Karen White (INTERNET COORDINATOR); Paul Fleetwood, Xiaoyun Wu (SYSTEMS)

President, The Mailbox Book Company™: Joseph C. Bucci
Director of Book Planning and Development: Chris Poindexter
Curriculum Director: Karen P. Shelton
Book Development Managers: Cayce Guiliano, Elizabeth H. Lindsay, Thad McLaurin

Editorial Planning: Kimberley Bruck (MANAGER); Debra Liverman, Sharon Murphy, Susan Walker (TEAM LEADERS)
Editorial and Freelance Management: Karen A. Brudnak; Sarah Hamblet, Hope Rodgers (EDITORIAL ASSISTANTS)
Editorial Production: Lisa K. Pitts (TRAFFIC MANAGER); Lynette Dickerson (TYPE SYSTEMS); Mark Rainey (TYPESETTER)
Librarian: Dorothy C. McKinney

More great science books from *The Mailbox*®:

TEC1458. The Best of *The Mailbox*® Science Made Simple • Preschool–Kindergarten

TEC1752. Quick & Easy Science Fun • Preschool–Kindergarten

About This Book

Welcome to *Investigating Science—Insects & Spiders*! This book is one of six must-have resource books that support the National Science Education Standards and are designed to supplement and enhance your existing science curriculum. Packed with practical cross-curricular ideas and thought-provoking reproducibles, these all-new, content-specific resource books provide preschool and kindergarten teachers with a collection of innovative and fun activities for teaching thematic science units.

Included in this book:
Investigating Science—Insects & Spiders contains five cross-curricular thematic units, each containing
- Background information for the teacher
- Easy-to-implement instructions for science experiments and projects
- Student-centered activities and reproducibles
- Literature links

Cross-curricular thematic units found in this book:
- *Insects*
- *Ants*
- *Honeybees*
- *Butterflies*
- *Spiders*

Other books in the preschool–kindergarten Investigating Science series:
- *Investigating Science—Plants*
- *Investigating Science—Five Senses*
- *Investigating Science—Animals*
- *Investigating Science—Taking Care of Me*
- *Investigating Science—Weather & the Seasons*

Insects

Give your youngsters a bug's-eye view of insects with the following ideas and reproducible activities!

Background for the Teacher

- An insect has a head, a thorax, an abdomen, and six legs.
- Most insects have two large compound eyes and three smaller ones.
- Most insects have one or two pairs of wings attached to their bodies.
- Most insects breathe through small holes in the sides of their abdomens and thoraxes.
- All insects hatch from eggs and often look completely different from the way they will look as adults.
- Many insects are helpful to plants, other animals, and people.

Books to Buzz About

Bugs! Bugs! Bugs! by Bob Barner
Buzz! A Book About Insects by Melvin Berger
Have You Seen Bugs? by Joanne Oppenheim
What Do Insects Do? by Susan Canizares
Where Do Insects Live? by Susan Canizares

Bug Bodies
(Art, Identifying the Parts of an Insect)

After participating in this puppet activity, your youngsters will be more familiar with the different parts of an insect. First, provide each child with a construction paper copy of page 8. Have him color and then cut out the dragonfly. Next, help him glue it to a craft stick to make an insect puppet. Then, as you describe a different part of an insect's body (see the list of suggestions on this page), ask each child to point to the corresponding body part. Call on a volunteer to name the part.

To further reinforce students' understanding of insect parts, provide each child with a copy of page 9. Have him cut out the bug pattern and cards. Next, pair students and provide each pair with a die. Have each player lay his cards faceup in front of him. In turn, have each child roll the die and color the corresponding insect part on the pattern. If a part is already colored, that child loses his turn. Have youngsters continue playing until both insects are colored.

- Found between the eyes, an insect uses these to smell, feel, taste, or hear. *(antennae)*
- All insects have six of these. *(legs)*
- Insects sometimes have sticky pads on these, which help the insects walk upside down. *(feet)*
- An insect uses these to fly and search for food or to escape from an enemy. *(wings)*
- An insect uses these to see. They can have thousands of lenses. *(eyes)*

It's All in the Legs
(Categorizing, Counting)

What's one sure way to tell the difference between an insect and a spider? Just count the legs! Insects have six legs and spiders have eight legs. Share this information with your little ones and then send them off to play this center game. In advance, gather two paper lunch bags. Label one bag "Spider" and draw a circle on the bottom. Label the other bag "Insect" and draw a square on the bottom. Next, make a construction paper copy of the cards on page 10. For easy self-checking, draw a circle on the back of each spider card and a square on the back of each insect card. Place the bags and the cards (faceup) at the center. To play, a student selects a card, counts the number of legs, decides whether the creature is an insect or spider, and then places it in the appropriate bag. Play continues in the same manner with the remaining cards. Afterward, the child empties each bag and matches the shapes to check her work.

Cricket Investigations
(Listening, Observing)

Help your students fine-tune their observation and listening skills with this activity. In advance, purchase several male crickets from a local bait shop or fishing supply store. Place them in a jar or plastic container with some grass or straw and a little water. Be sure to poke several airholes in the lid.

Place the crickets in an area of the classroom away from direct sunlight. During a specified time of the day, invite youngsters to observe the crickets. Discuss their behavior and listen for chirping. To encourage chirping, place a dark cloth over the jar. Explain to students that crickets are most active in the evening, and covering the jar tricks them into believing it's nighttime, making them more likely to chirp. As students observe, encourage them to share what they would like to learn about crickets. List their questions on a sheet of chart paper. During your study, encourage youngsters to answer the questions through observation. Research any unanswered questions and share the results with students. *Cricketology* by Michael Elsohn Ross is a great resource about finding, collecting, and keeping crickets. Then, provide each child with a preassembled copy of the minibooklet on pages 11–12 and have him color each page. After reading the minibooklet together, encourage each student to take his home to share with family. At the end of your study, be sure to release the crickets.

Our Cricket Questions
How far can they jump?
How do they make the chirping noise?
What food do they like to eat?
Can crickets swim?

Male or Female?
An adult cricket has wings that are almost as long as its abdomen. A female has a long ovipositor (egg-laying tube). A male has upper wings that look like large fiddles. Rubbing these wings together causes the singing sound we associate with crickets.

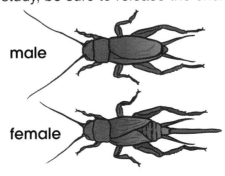

male

female

Eating on the Move
(Investigating the Eating Habits of a Ladybug)

Your youngsters will delight in this spin on the eating habits of ladybugs. Read to students *Are You a Ladybug?* by Judy Allen. Explain that because aphids feed on healthy plants, ladybugs help the plants survive by eating the aphids. Then guide your children through the steps below to illustrate a ladybug eating aphids.

Materials for each student:
white construction paper copy of page 13
brad
2 wiggle eyes
glue
scissors

Steps:
1. Color and cut out the patterns.
2. Glue the wiggle eyes onto the ladybug where indicated.
3. Connect the ladybug to the center of the leaf with the brad where indicated.
4. Turn the ladybug to show it eating the aphids.

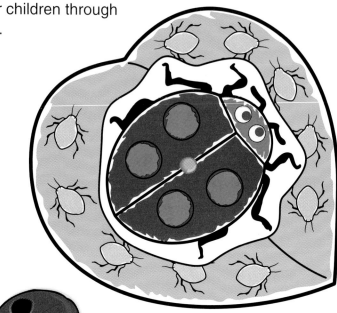

All the Aphids
(Song)

Put the ladybugs created in "Eating on the Move" to work! Ask students to turn the ladybug to eat one aphid at a time as they sing this counting song.

Aphids, Aphids
(sung to the tune of "Bicycle Built for Two")

Aphids, aphids
Crawling all around.
1, 2, 3, 4, 5
They're moving up and down.
Oh no! Oh no! What do I see?
You know, I have a hunch.
A ladybug,
A ladybug
Will eat you all for lunch!

Aphids, aphids
Crawling all around.
6, 7, 8, 9, 10
Ladybugs eat again.
Oh no! Oh no! What do I see?
You know, I have a hunch.
A ladybug,
A ladybug
Will eat you all for lunch!

Insects Galore!
(Categorizing, Graphing)

Students are sure to have some fun with this super sorting activity! In advance, gather a supply of index cards and a variety of plastic insects and spiders. Place the insects and spiders in a large container. Seat your youngsters and scatter the insects and spiders on the floor. Choose categories such as "insects" and "not insects." Label index cards accordingly and place one on each side of the pile. Challenge students to categorize each creature. Remind the children that an insect has six legs; therefore, those creatures should be placed in the insects section. Other creatures should be placed in the "not insects" section. Afterward, draw a simple chart on the board to record the results. Continue in this same manner with other categories, such as number of legs, shape, antennae, and size. Wow—there are a lot of insects!

Insects in Our World
(Song)

Here's a catchy tune to help review the importance of insects in our world! Teach your youngsters the verses below. Once students have mastered these verses, enlist their help in creating more verses to describe different insects. How many insects can your little bug-watchers sing about? Bet there are plenty!

Itsy-Bitsy Helpers
(sung to the tune of "The Itsy-Bitsy Spider")

Itsy-bitsy helpers, you help us every day.
What would we do if you ever went away?

Bees give us honey, and ants work very hard.
Ladybugs eat aphids and leave a pretty yard.

Itsy-bitsy helpers, you help us every day.
What would we do if you ever went away?

Butterflies eat nectar and taste with their feet.
Grasshoppers eat leaves, and their jumping can't be beat!

Itsy-bitsy helpers, you help us every day.
What would we do if you ever went away?

Crickets give us music that makes us want to sing.
Oh, itsy-bitsy helpers, you do so many things!

Dragonfly Pattern
Use with "Bug Bodies" on page 4.

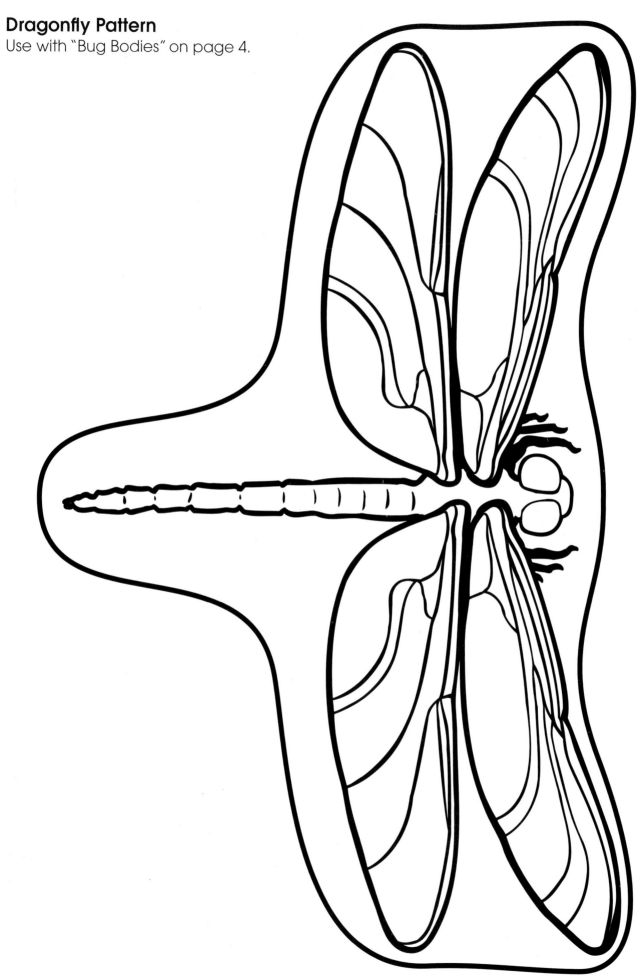

eyes

antennae

legs

body

wings

head

Insect and Spider Cards

Use with "It's All in the Legs" on page 5.

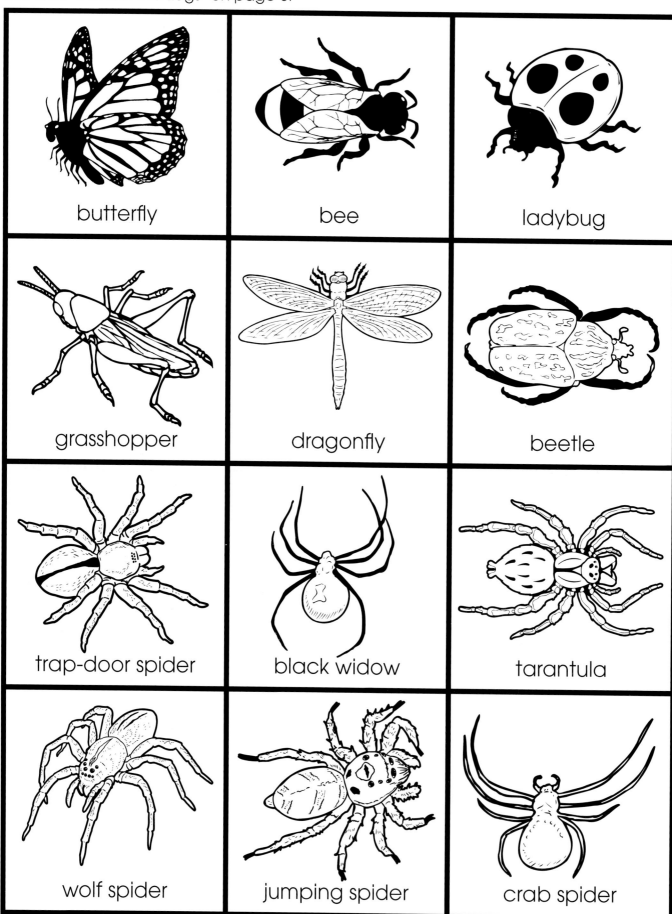

butterfly

bee

ladybug

grasshopper

dragonfly

beetle

trap-door spider

black widow

tarantula

wolf spider

jumping spider

crab spider

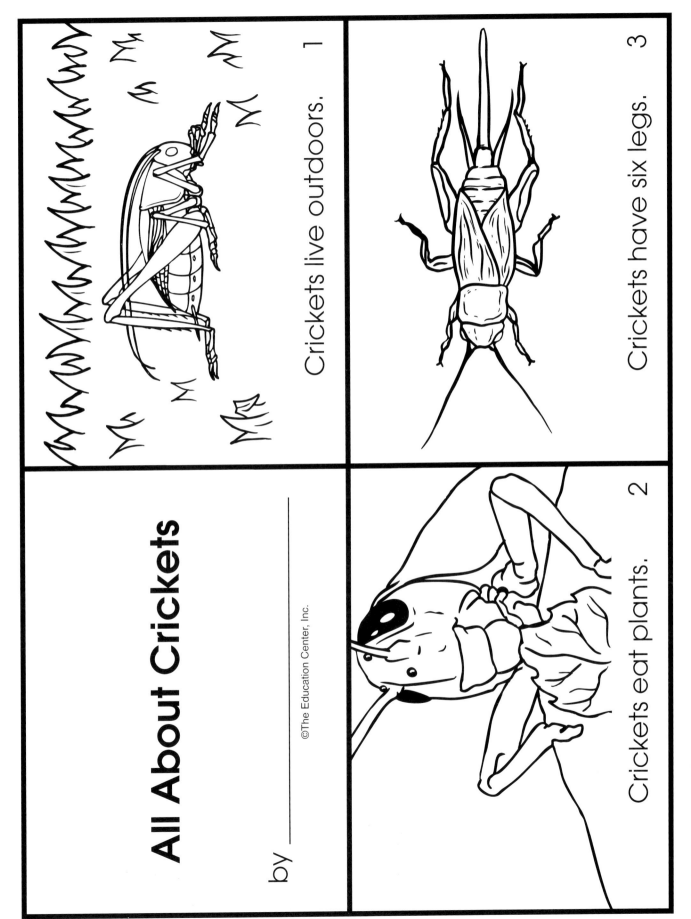

1

Crickets live outdoors.

3

Crickets have six legs.

All About Crickets

by _____

©The Education Center, Inc.

2

Crickets eat plants.

Booklet Pages
Use with "Cricket Investigations" on page 5.

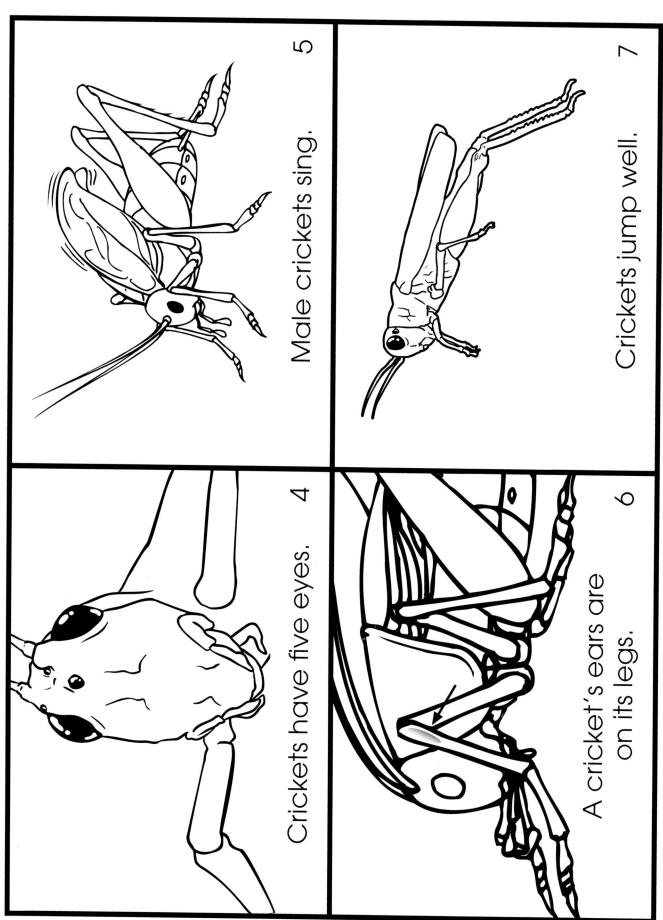

5

Male crickets sing.

7

Crickets jump well.

4

Crickets have five eyes.

6

A cricket's ears are on its legs.

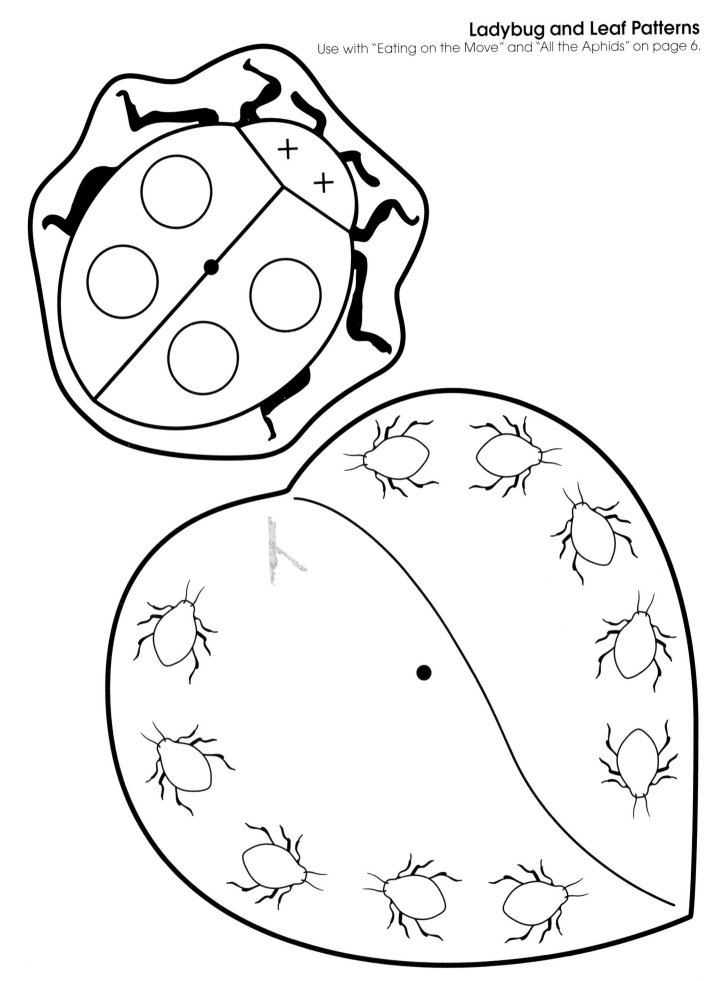

Ants

Although ants have a reputation for being pesky visitors, the following activities show students that these insects are quite amazing!

Background for the Teacher

- Ants live in organized colonies. An anthill can have hundreds of separate rooms!
- Ants can give off aromas that signal other ants, telling where food can be found or other information. The other ants follow the scent to the food.
- In most species, male ants and young queen ants have wings.
- Queen ants shed their wings soon after mating.
- Ants are very strong. If an ant were your size, it could lift a small car!

"Brilli-ant" Books

Ant Cities by Arthur Dorros
Ants by Ruth Berman
Are You an Ant? by Judy Allen
Thinking About Ants by Barbara Brenner

Follow That Trail!
(Investigating Ants)

Follow the trail (of yarn, that is!) to an ant-style picnic. While your youngsters are out of the room, divide a class supply of individually packaged snacks into five groups and hide each in a different part of your classroom. Then place five different-colored skeins of yarn in your circle area.

When students return, seat them in your circle area and tell them that ants leave invisible chemical trails to help other ants in the colony find food. Next, explain to students that they are going to pretend to be ants. Divide your students into five small groups to represent colonies. Designate one child in each colony to represent the scout, two others to be workers, and the rest to be ants waiting in the anthill. Tell the scouts that their job is to find food for the colony and then provide a trail so the worker ants can get the food. Direct each scout to take a skein of yarn and search for a group of snacks. When he finds the food, he unwinds the yarn to leave a trail from the food to the colony. Then the worker ants follow the trail to find the food and bring it back to the colony. Encourage each ant to enjoy a picnic-style snack. Afterward, regroup your little ones for a discussion about the activity. Tell students that just as each group had its own color of yarn, it is believed that ants from each colony deposit their own unique chemical smell. This helps keep ants from getting mixed in with other colonies. "Ant-astic!"

Ants in Action
(Observing, Communicating)

Your youngsters are sure to enjoy watching ants build tunnels in this homemade ant habitat! In advance, obtain an empty, clean two-liter plastic soda bottle with the top cut off. Fill it half full with lightly moistened potting soil. Poke a few holes into the soil with a skewer or thick stick to help the ants establish tunnels. Search for ants on a playground or sidewalk around the school. To safely gather the ants, lay down a sheet of paper and wait for several ants to crawl onto it. Transfer them into the bottle by gently shaking the paper. Be careful not to mix ants from different colonies. Cover the top of the bottle with a piece of gauze and secure it with a rubber band. Place the habitat away from direct sunlight.

To feed the ants, mix a small amount of honey and water. Give them a few drops of the mixture in a milk jug lid every few days. Lightly mist the soil with water and introduce a solid food source once a week, such as a dead fly or a peanut. Be sure to remove unused food, as it will spoil. Allow time for students to observe the colony over the next several weeks. Provide a copy of the observation sheet on page 17, crayons, and magnifying glasses. Encourage students to draw and write about their observations. Bind the observation sheets into a class book titled "Our Ants in Action." At the completion of your study, return the ants to their original colony.

Ant Anatomy

(Formulating Models, Identification)

As a special treat for your hardworking youngsters, help them assemble these edible ants, which will also teach them about the basic body parts of ants. In advance, gather a napkin, three Mini Oreo cookies, eight chow mein noodles, two chocolate chips, and a dab of chocolate frosting for each child. Show pictures of ants and point out their three body segments (head, thorax, and abdomen), six legs, two antennae, and two eyes. Then provide each child with the materials listed above. Help each student construct an ant as shown. Help her use the frosting to join the three body segments together and to attach the eyes to the head. Then have her insert the legs and antennae into the cream in the cookies. Ask her to count the legs, eyes, and antennae of her ant and tell which segment each one is connected to. Then invite her to eat and enjoy!

15

Fast Food
(Demonstration, Game)

After learning about ants, give students the opportunity to act like them! To prepare, place several items of varying sizes and shapes in two equal piles. Objects may include boxes, balls, stuffed toys, pencils, and books. Some objects should be small and light, others large and heavy. Divide the children into two teams. Provide each team with two sets of kitchen tongs and assign each team a pile of items. The goal for each team is to use the tongs to transport its items to a designated point across the room. As the game progresses, some students may realize that it will take two students to transport some of the objects. The first team to transport all of its objects across the room is the winner.

When the race is over, discuss how using the tongs was similar to how ants transport goods. *(They use their jaws to carry food and building materials.)* Also talk about how students had to work together as a team to get a difficult job done. Help them compare that to the teamwork displayed by ants in their colonies.

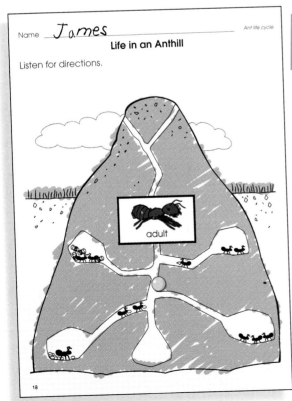

Name James   Ant life cycle
Life in an Anthill

Listen for directions.

18

Life in an Anthill
(Creating a Model)

Illustrate the ant life cycle with this interactive anthill! In advance, duplicate page 18 and the life cycle patterns on page 19 to make a class supply. Gather youngsters and read aloud *Ant Cities* by Arthur Dorros. Revisit pages 12–14 in the book and discuss with students how ants hatch as larvae from eggs laid by the queen, change into pupae, and then emerge as adult ants ready to work in the anthill. Give each child a copy of page 18 and the life cycle patterns. Then guide your youngsters to cut out the wheel and color and cut out the life cycle pictures. Help each child glue the pictures in order on the wheel and set it aside to dry. Then encourage each child to lightly color the anthill on his copy of page 18. Help him cut out the window and place the wheel behind it so the dots are aligned. Have him fasten the wheel behind the anthill with a brad. To complete the activity, have each child gently turn his wheel as he explains the ant life cycle to a partner.

Ants in Action!

I see _____ ants.

They are _____.

Here is what they look like:

Life in an Anthill

Listen for directions.

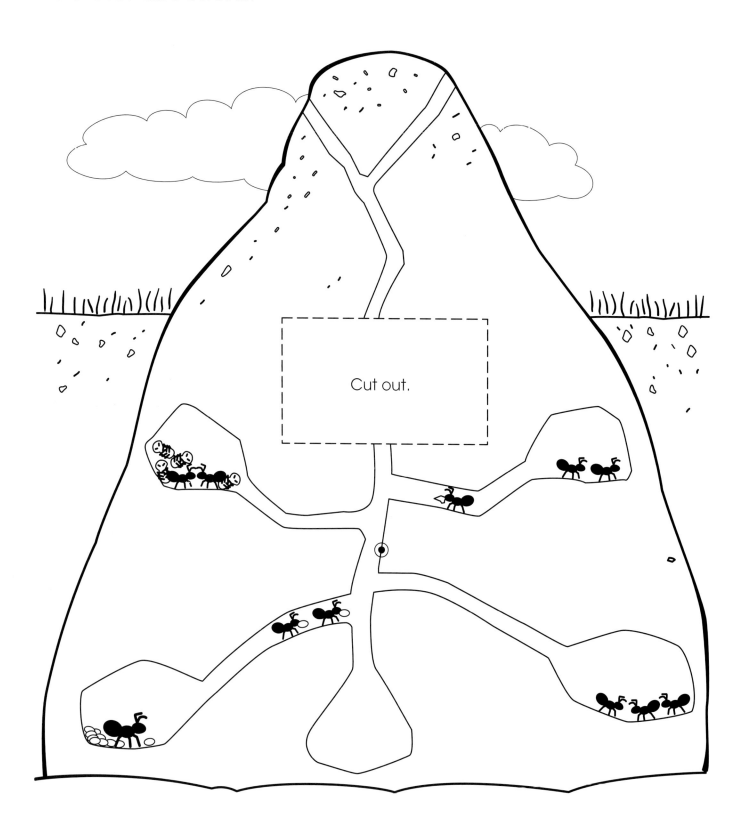

Cut out.

Note to the teacher: Use with "Life in an Anthill" on page 16.

life cycle pictures

wheel

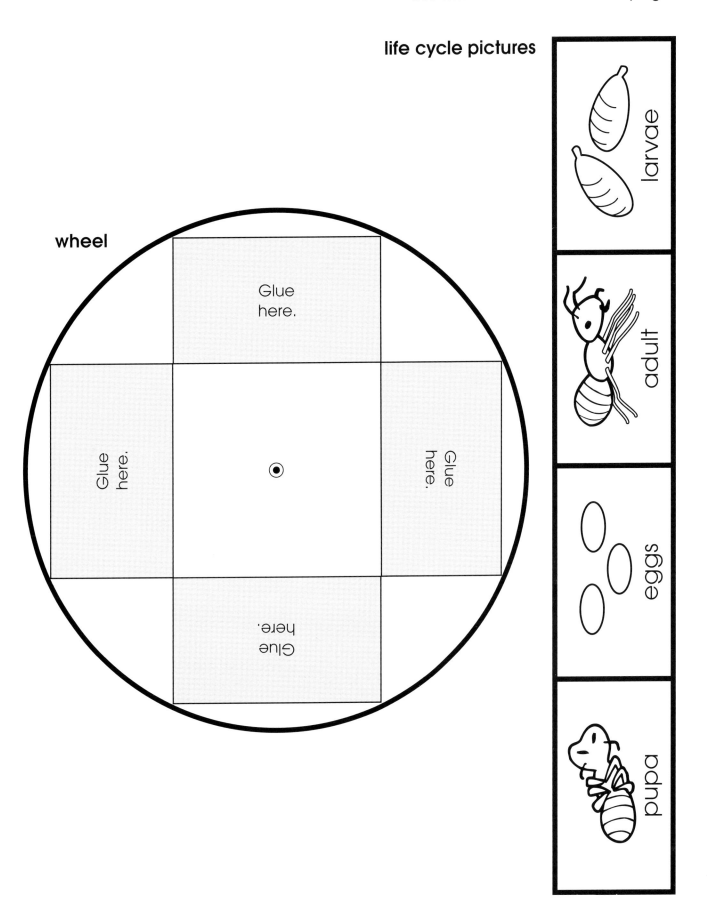

Glue here.

Glue here.

Glue here.

Glue here.

larvae

adult

eggs

pupa

Honeybees

Your hive will be abuzz with lots of sweet learning.

Background for the Teacher

- Bees collect pollen and nectar from flowers for food.
- Each worker bee who forages for food gathers pollen and nectar from as many as 10,000 flowers a day.
- Honeybees produce honey from nectar.
- Honeybee hives contain honeycombs, which are made of six-sided compartments called cells.
- Honeybees have two antennae, four wings, six legs, three main body parts (head, thorax, and abdomen), and a mouth. Female bees have a stinger, which is used for defense.
- Each bee colony has one queen.
- Male bees are called drones. The unmated female bees are called worker bees.

Buzzing Good Books!

From Flower to Honey by Robin Nelson
Honeybees by Deborah Heiligman
Honey Bees and Flowers by Lola M. Schaefer
The Honey Makers by Gail Gibbons

Foraging Fun
(Role-Playing)

Use this hands-on activity to help your youngsters understand how hard bees work to gather food. While students are away from the classroom, hide artificial flowers in various spots around the room. Place a handful of yellow pom-poms next to each hidden flower to represent pollen and nectar. Put an empty basket in the center of the room to represent the beehive.

When students return, explain that worker honeybees forage (search) for pollen and nectar and then bring it back to the hive, where it is stored for food. Then invite each child to pretend to be a bee and walk around the room, searching for pollen and nectar. When a child locates a flower, he should bring one pom-pom back to the hive and then go search for a new flower. When all the pom-poms are collected, have students observe how much pollen and nectar is in the basket. Discuss what it would be like to spend an entire day finding and carrying pollen and nectar. Conclude the activity by explaining that lots of bees work together to feed the hive. In her entire life, a honeybee collects only enough nectar to create about one teaspoon of honey. Wow, that's a lot of hard work!

These easy-to-make models are the bee's knees! In advance, obtain a golf ball–size lump of yellow Crayola Model Magic modeling compound for each child. Cut nine two-inch lengths of brown pipe cleaner for each child. Also cut a class supply of four-inch white paper squares.

Discuss with students the parts of a honeybee's body, using a photo as a guide. Help them notice the main body parts (head, thorax, and abdomen) and interesting features, such as two pairs of wings, two antennae, six legs, and a stinger. Don't forget to draw students' attention to the proboscis, or hollow tongue. Then give each child a portion of modeling compound and encourage him to shape it into a head, thorax, and abdomen. Invite him to pinch the end of the abdomen into a point to resemble a stinger. Have him insert three pipe cleaner sections into each side of the thorax to represent legs as shown. Next, instruct him to insert two pipe cleaner sections into the head to resemble antennae. Help him insert the last pipe cleaner section into the head to resemble the bee's tongue. Set the models aside to dry overnight. The next day, have each child use a black marker to draw eyes on the head and stripes on the abdomen. Then help him cut four wings from white paper and glue them in pairs onto the thorax. When the models are completely dry, invite students to compare them to photographs or commercial models of honeybees. Bet there's plenty to buzz about!

Honeybees build honeycombs with hexagonal cells. Each wall is an equal, straight line, so each cell joins evenly to the next. Use this activity to illustrate how hexagons neatly fit together to form a comb. To prepare, make a class supply of page 25 and set the copies aside. Gather a quantity of hexagonal pattern blocks and round poker chips. During a group time, show the manipulatives to the students. Ask them to predict which shape bees would prefer to use for a honeycomb cell. Then have a volunteer try to fit each type of shape together to form a comb. Discuss the appearance of each resulting comb. Lead students to notice any wasted space or gaps between cells and to conclude that hexagons fit together better than circles. Then give each child a copy of page 25 and invite her to make her own honeycomb. Direct each child to carefully cut out the shapes and fit them together on the honeycomb. When she is satisfied with her comb, invite her to glue the shapes in place. Display the completed sheets for a long-lasting reminder of honeycombs and hexagons.

What a Busy Bee!
(Making a Booklet)

It's no secret—worker honeybees stay busy! Help youngsters understand all the different jobs a worker bee performs during her lifetime with this interactive booklet. To begin, make a class supply of pages 26–29 on white construction paper. Cut a ten-inch length of yarn for each child. Have each child color and cut out her booklet cover and pages, pocket, and bee manipulative. To assemble the booklet, help each child stack her pages, in order, behind the cover. Help her staple them along the left side. Next, instruct her to glue the pocket to the back of page 7. (Make sure she doesn't accidentally glue the pocket closed.) Help her tape one end of the yarn above the pocket and the other end to the back of the bee. Then have her write her name on the cover of her booklet. Read through the booklet with students, modeling how to use the bee manipulative as a pointer on each page. Then encourage each child to store her bee manipulative in the pocket.

Live From the Hive
(Dramatic Play)

Youngsters will make a beeline to this exciting dramatic-play center! After students have completed the "What a Busy Bee!" booklets (above), invite them to use dramatic play to strengthen their understanding. In advance, set up an area similar to the one shown to resemble a beehive. Create a background by hanging lengths of yellow bulletin board paper. Provide brown crayons for students to draw honeycomb cells on the paper. Also set out paper cups to represent honeycomb cells that students can fill with larvae (white cotton balls) and collected pollen. Near the center, scatter artificial flowers and yellow pom-poms to represent pollen. Before opening the center, revisit with students the various jobs of a worker bee, from cleaning cells to collecting food. Then encourage visitors to this center to act out the roles of various worker bees in a honeybee hive.

Did you know that forager bees communicate the location of new flowers through dance? Give your youngsters a chance to try out this bee-style dance. To represent the bees' circle dance (indicating nearby flowers), have students stand in a circle. Play some lively music and invite students to follow you as you dance around the circle. When you reach your starting point, have students pause; then turn and dance around the circle in the opposite direction. Repeat as desired, making sure to switch directions with each revolution. To represent the bees' wag-tail dance (indicating distant flowers), have students stand in a line in a large, open area. (If desired, play more lively music.) Lead students to wiggle as they walk in a straight line; then walk normally as you form a semicircle around the wiggle line. Wiggle-walk along the straight line again; then walk in a semicircle on the other side of the line to form a figure eight as shown. Repeat as desired, making sure to keep the figure eight wide enough for all students to safely walk. That's it! Do the hive jive!

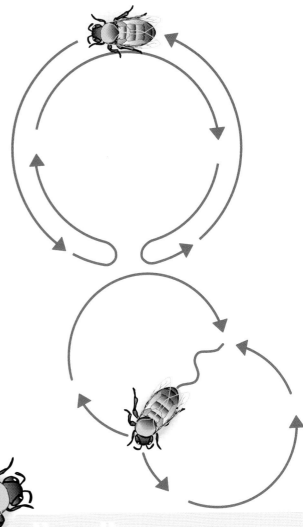

This adorable fingerplay will help youngsters recall how and why bees make honey. Discuss with students how a forager bee brings nectar back to the hive to make honey. Remind them that honey is the bees' food. Then teach your students the rhyme and hand movements below. Repeat this fingerplay throughout your bee study for some sweet fun!

One little honeybee,	*Hold up one finger.*
Buzzing all around,	*Make circular motion with finger.*
Spies a little flower	*Hold hand to forehead and look around.*
Growing from the ground.	*Push hand through opposite fist to represent growing flower.*
Sipping lots of nectar	
With her long, long tongue,	*Wiggle index finger.*
She brings it to her hive	*Make flying motion with index finger.*
To feed the hungry young.	*Wiggle fingers on opposite hand to represent baby bees.*
This tasty treat called honey	*Rub tummy.*
Is made by honeybees.	
And if we treat them kindly,	*Put hand on heart.*
They'll share with you and me!	*Point to another child and self.*

"Bee-dazzling" Flowers
(Making a Model)

People and bees see colors very differently. Humans do not see ultraviolet light, but bees do. This remarkable light is reflected off special markings found on flower petals. These paths lead the bees to the sweet nectar inside the flower. This activity will help your little ones understand the difference between how bees see flowers and how people see flowers. To prepare, cut a 6" x 9" sheet of waxed paper for each child. Give each child a sheet of white paper and invite her to draw and color a large, simple flower in the center. Have her write "This is what I see" on the left side of the paper. Then help her place the waxed paper over the right half of the flower and tape it in place as shown. Supervise the child as she uses a permanent marker to trace the flower's outline on the waxed paper. Next, have her draw vein lines on the petals to represent the ultraviolet light paths. Support as needed while she writes "This is like what a bee sees" on the waxed paper. Display the finished models on a bulletin board and discuss the different types of flowers and paths.

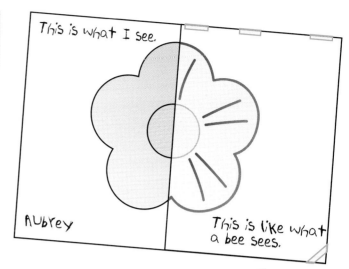

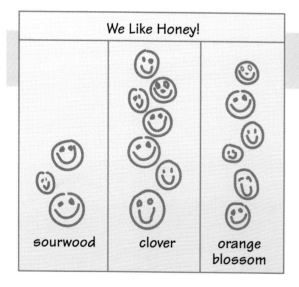

How Sweet It Is!
(Taste Test, Collecting Data, Graphing)

Honeybees collect nectar and pollen from many types of flowers. Each type of nectar influences the resulting honey's taste. Find out which flavor of honey your students like best with this tasty graphing activity! To prepare, purchase crackers and three different types of honey. Set up three honey-tasting stations with a class supply of crackers and a small dish of honey at each. Label a three-column graph with the three types of honey.

Invite each child to visit each station and sample the honey. Encourage him to secretly decide which flavor is his favorite. When each child has sampled each kind of honey, show students the graph. Invite each child, in turn, to draw a smiley face in the column that represents his preferred honey flavor. Discuss the completed graph and post it in your classroom for a sweet display.

24

Hive Builders

Cut. Build. Glue.

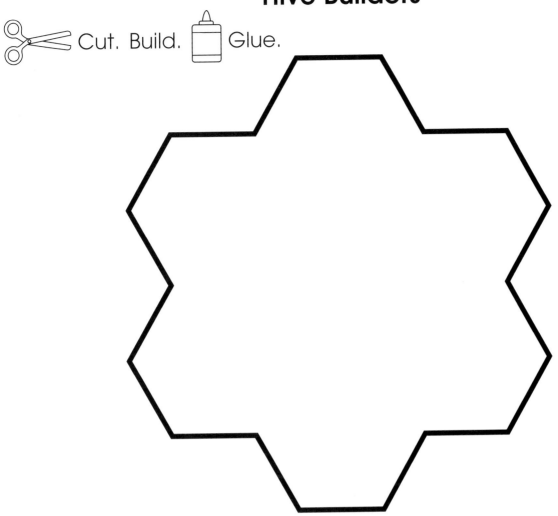

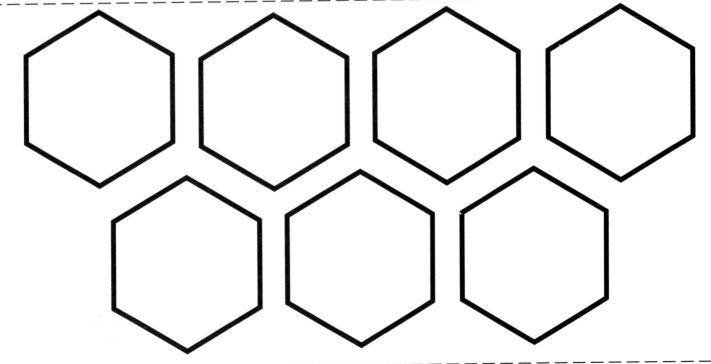

Note to the teacher: Use with "Hive Builders" on page 21.

1

A new worker bee has emerged.

bee

What a Busy Bee!

by _____

©The Education Center, Inc.

Staple here.

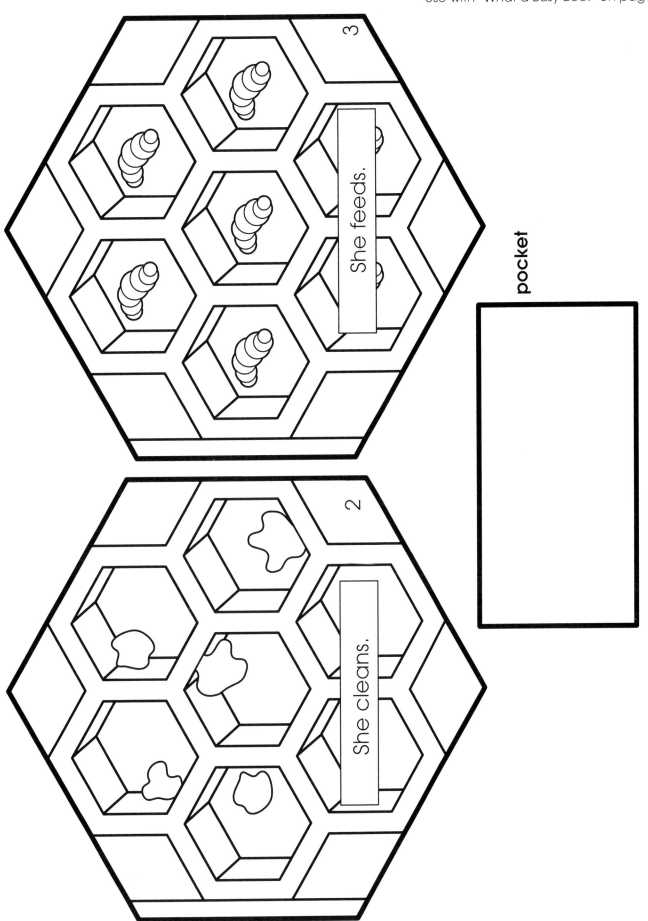

3

She feeds.

pocket

2

She cleans.

Booklet Pages 4 and 5

Use with "What a Busy Bee!" on page 22.

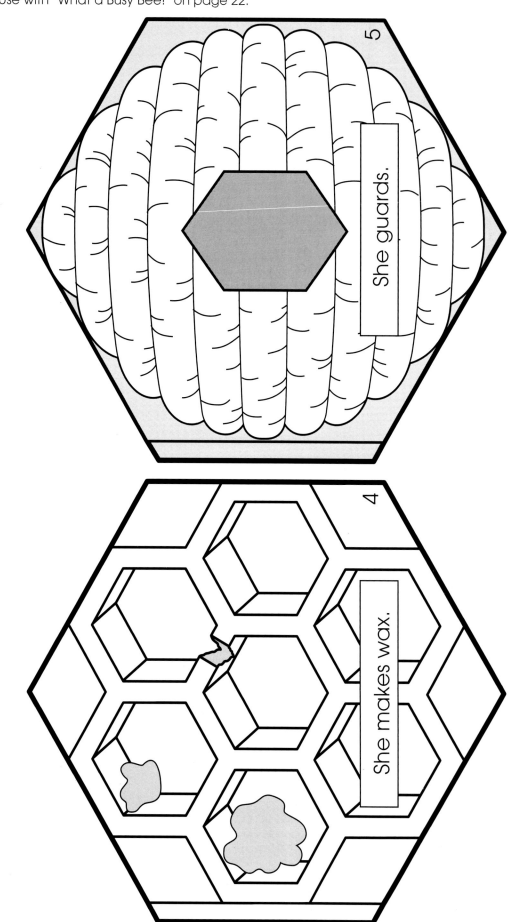

5

She guards.

4

She makes wax.

7

What a busy bee!

6

She finds food.

Butterflies

These butterfly-related activities will fascinate your youngsters and leave them with a flutter in their hearts!

Background for the Teacher

- Butterflies metamorphose through four stages: egg, larva, pupa, and adult.
- Butterflies live in most parts of the world. During winter in colder regions, they must hibernate or migrate to warmer climates.
- The size of a butterfly's wings and body determines how it will fly.
- Many butterflies have colors that keep them from harm and allow them to blend into their surroundings.
- Butterflies belong to the group of insects called Lepidoptera.

Flutter Books

Butterfly House by Eve Bunting
Crinkleroot's Guide to Knowing Butterflies and Moths by Jim Arnosky
From Caterpillar to Butterfly by Deborah Heiligman
Life Cycle of a Butterfly by Angela Royston
Monarch Butterfly by Gail Gibbons
Waiting for Wings by Lois Ehlert

Perfect Parts
(Identifying Butterfly Body Parts)

Introduce your little ones to the various parts of a butterfly with this flannelboard activity! To prepare, duplicate page 34 to make a class supply. Also enlarge a copy of page 34 onto white construction paper or tagboard. Color the butterfly body parts on the enlarged copy. Then cut out the body parts and labels and prepare them for flannelboard use. Store the cutouts in a basket near your flannelboard. During a group time, gather youngsters around the flannelboard. Assemble the butterfly as you describe and name each body part. Encourage a volunteer to disassemble the butterfly and then describe the parts as he reassembles it. Follow up by giving each child a copy of page 34. Provide support as each child cuts and glues to label the butterfly's body parts. Oh, so *that's* a thorax!

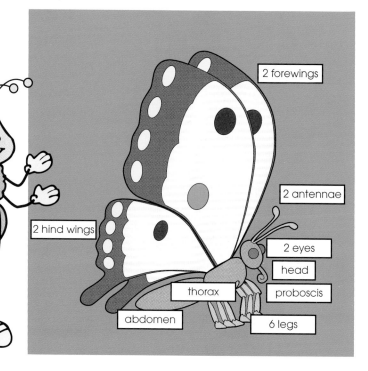

Butterfly Math
(Counting Sets of Two)

Butterflies have two antennae, so they're perfect to help your little ones learn to count by twos. To begin, copy page 35 to make a class supply. Give each child in a small group a copy of page 35 and a pencil. Have her turn her sheet over and use the available space to draw a butterfly's wings and body. Then ask the group how many antennae a butterfly has. Encourage each child to add two antennae to the butterfly's head. Have her number them to help reinforce the concept. Then have each child turn her sheet over, count the antennae of the first pictured butterfly, and write the corresponding number in the box. Offer support as needed while students complete the sheet. Point out that each time the number of butterflies increases by one, the number of antennae increases by two. Encourage students to predict the next number before counting. For a more challenging activity, provide Unifix cubes and have students make sets of two and then practice counting by twos to a desired number, such as 20. Two, four, six, eight—butterflies are really great!

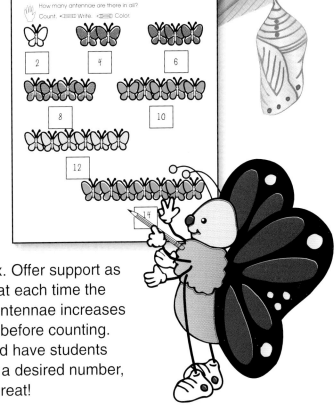

A Beautiful Butterfly
(Exploring Growth and Change)

A caterpillar sure changes a lot! Make these marvelous metamorphosis booklets with youngsters to illustrate the process. In advance, copy pages 36–39 to make a class supply. After reading a nonfiction book about butterfly metamorphosis, discuss the different stages of a butterfly's life with your students. Then have each child cut apart his booklet cover and pages. Have him follow the directions below to decorate each page. Afterward, help him sequence his pages and staple them along the left side. Encourage each child to take his booklet home to share with his family.

Materials for each child: copy of pages 36–39, scissors, access to a stapler and hole puncher, crayons, glue, craft stick, black marker, 6" x 4" sheet of green construction paper, brown paint, white scrap paper

Page-Decorating Instructions
Cover: Write your name on the line. Color the butterfly.
Page 1: Color the leaf green. Punch one white dot; then glue it to the leaf.
Page 2: Color the craft stick green; then use a black marker to draw stripes. Glue it to the page.

Page 3: Fold the green construction paper in half and cut two leaf shapes. Punch three holes in the first leaf and glue it to the page.
Page 4: Punch ten holes in the second leaf cutout and glue it to the page.
Page 5: Color the branch brown. Make one brown fingerprint on the center of the branch to resemble a chrysalis.
Page 6: Repeat the process from page 5, adding "Zzzzz" to indicate the changing caterpillar in the resting stage.
Page 7: Color the butterfly.

31

Caterpillar Snack
(Tasting Leaves)

Caterpillars can be picky eaters. For example, monarch caterpillars prefer to eat the leaves of milkweed plants. Children can also be picky eaters, but a little imagination can make this leafy snack a big hit! In advance, purchase a bottle of ranch salad dressing. Also purchase a variety of salad greens and prepare each type for eating. Place each type of green in a separate bowl with a pair of salad tongs (or a plastic fork). Explain to your students that caterpillars eat different kinds of leaves, and people do too! Further explain that the special leaves people eat are lettuce and other salad greens; then provide each child with a paper cup or bowl, a plastic fork, and a napkin. Invite each child to pretend to be a caterpillar choosing tasty green leaves to munch. When each child has chosen some salad greens, offer him a squirt of dressing, and encourage him to dig in. Crunch, crunch, caterpillars munch!

Watch Me Grow
(Understanding the Butterfly Life Cycle, Making a Model)

Metamorphosis is fascinating! Engage your little ones with this artistic life cycle wheel. In advance, gather a small lump of white Crayola Model Magic compound, a paper plate, a small white baby lima bean (or pom-pom), a section of white chenille bump stem, and a four-inch square of colorful construction paper for each child. To begin, have each child shape her modeling compound into a chrysalis shape and set it aside to dry. Then invite her to paint the back of her paper plate green with washable tempera paint. When the paint is dry, help her use a black marker to draw lines on the plate to visually divide it into quarters as shown. Have her glue the bean on the first quadrant to represent the butterfly's egg. Have her glue the chenille bump stem section on the next quadrant to resemble the newly hatched caterpillar. Next, help her glue the chrysalis on the third quadrant. Then help her fold the construction paper in half, draw a butterfly half on the crease, and cut it out to form a butterfly. Help each child glue the crease of the butterfly to the last blank space on the wheel. Encourage each child to use her wheel to explain the butterfly life cycle to a classmate. If desired, add more challenge by directing each child to label her wheel. Wow, that's a "wheel-y" good life cycle model!

Work, Work, Work
(Song, Role-Playing)

Explore through dramatic play and song the important job butterflies perform. Seat youngsters in a circle and explain that butterflies help some flowering plants by spreading pollen from one plant to another. Plants must have pollen to make seeds for new plants. Further explain that as a butterfly drinks nectar from a flower, pollen sticks to its body. Then the butterfly carries the pollen to other flowers. Next, teach students the song below. Select a volunteer to pretend to be a butterfly while the rest of the class pretends to be flowers. As the group sings, encourage the butterfly to move among the flowers, gently touching each on the head as if spreading pollen from flower to flower. Select a new butterfly and repeat the song. Continue in this manner as long as interest dictates.

I'm a Little Butterfly
(sung to the tune of "I'm a Little Teapot")

I'm a little butterfly flying round,
Spreading the pollen I have found.
From flower to flower I will go,
Helping flowers grow, grow, grow!

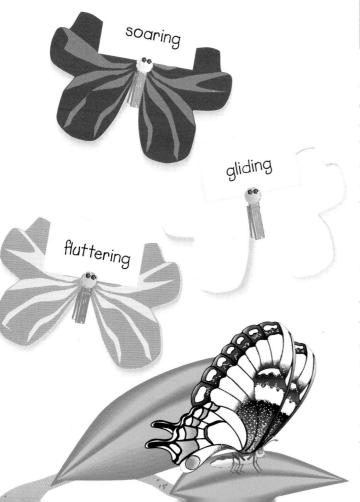

soaring

gliding

fluttering

Magical Movements
(Using Descriptive Language, Craft)

Gliding, soaring—there are many ways to describe the gentle movements of a butterfly. This creative activity will help your students learn to use descriptive language. To begin, provide each child with crayons or markers, a clothespin, a large colored pom-pom, a pair of tiny black pom-poms for eyes, glue, an index card, and a sheet of colored tissue paper. Have each child color the clothespin to resemble a butterfly's body and then glue the large pom-pom to the bottom as shown. Next, have her glue the eyes to the large pom-pom to complete the butterfly's head. Help each child accordion-fold her tissue paper and pinch the center with the clothespin to give the butterfly wings. Then encourage each child to "fly" her butterfly while thinking of words that describe the butterfly's movement. Help her write one of her words on an index card and carefully pinch it with the clothespin as shown. Display the descriptive butterflies on a bulletin board. Conclude the activity by inviting each child to read her word aloud. Flitter, flutter, butterfly!

33

Perfect Parts

Cut.
Label.
Glue.

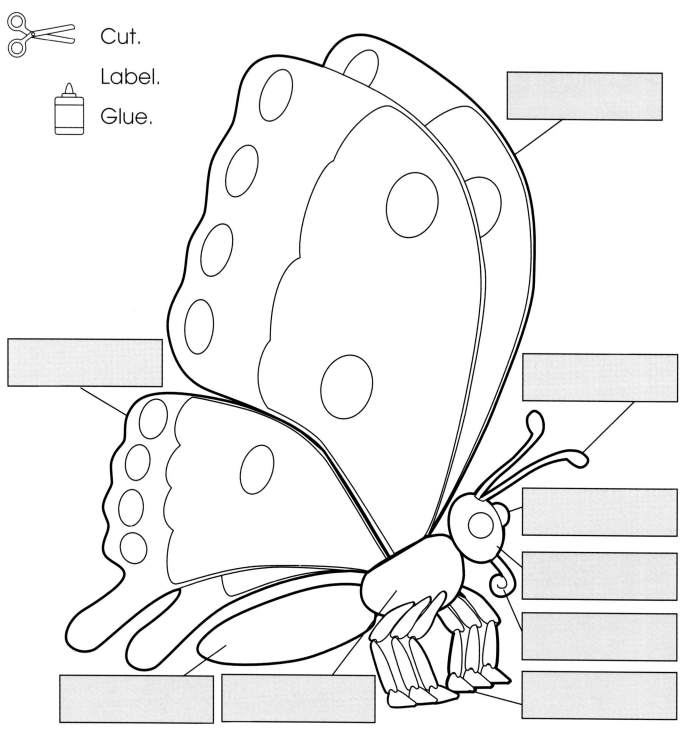

head	thorax	abdomen
2 forewings	2 hind wings	6 legs
proboscis	2 antennae	2 eyes

Butterfly Antennae

 How many antennae are there in all?

Count. ✏ Write. 🖍 Color.

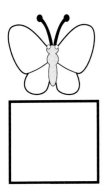

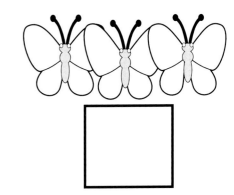

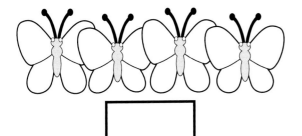

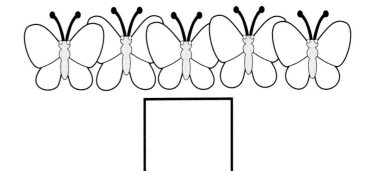

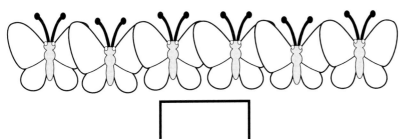

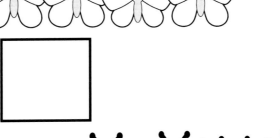

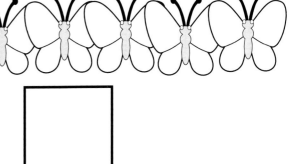

Note to the Teacher: Use with "Butterfly Math" on page 31.

A Beautiful Butterfly

Name _____

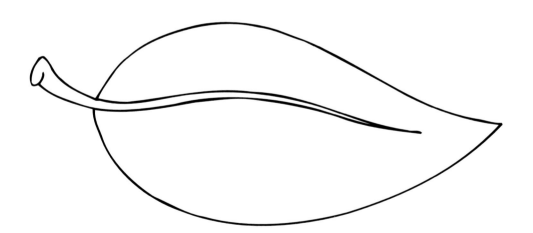

First, a tiny egg can be seen.

1

Next, there's a caterpillar, striped and green.   2

He eats and eats. Munch, munch, munch!   3

He eats some more.
Crunch, crunch, crunch!

4

Soon it's time to take a rest.
A chrysalis will work the best.

5

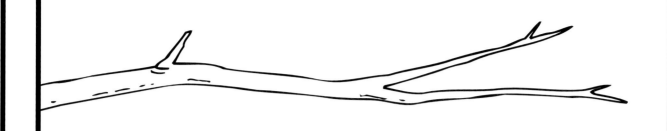

He'll sleep and sleep deep inside
Until he can no longer hide.

6

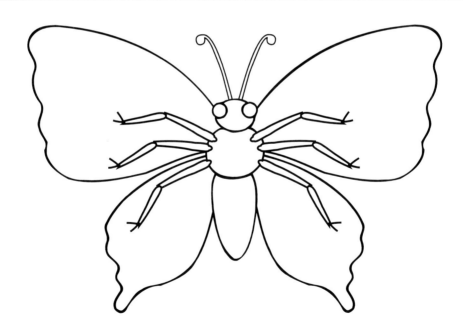

Then out pops a beautiful butterfly,
Just waiting for his wings to dry.

7

Spiders

Lure your little ones into a wonderful web of learning with this awesome collection of arachnid activities!

Background for the Teacher

- Spiders are arachnids, a group of invertebrates that have two body sections (abdomen and cephalothorax) and eight legs.
- All spiders can spin silk. About half of all spiders spin webs.
- Tarantulas and trap-door spiders can live to be 20 years old!
- A spider has a hard exoskeleton to protect its body. The exoskeleton does not grow, so it must be shed periodically as the spider gets larger.
- A spider's enemies include birds, snakes, frogs, lizards, wasps, and many other animals.

Arachnid Reading

I Didn't Know That Spiders Have Fangs by Claire Llewellyn
The Life Cycle of a Spider by Bobbie Kalman and Kathryn Smithyman
Mighty Spiders! by Fay Robinson
Sophie's Masterpiece by Eileen Spinelli
Spiders Spin Webs by Yvonne Winer
The Spider Weaver: A Legend of Kente Cloth by Margaret Musgrove

Amazing Spider Anatomy
(Identifying Spider Anatomy, Making a Model)

Legs, fangs, and eyes, oh my! Use this activity to introduce your youngsters to the amazing anatomy of the spider! In advance, make a class supply of the spider pattern at the top of page 44 and gather the materials listed below. To begin the activity, explain that spiders have eight legs, two body sections, and fangs, although very few ever bite people. Spiders can also have two, four, six, or eight eyes. Further explain that almost all spiders spin a silk dragline that keeps them anchored to a surface when they drop down. Next, distribute the materials below and guide each child through the steps to create a spider model. When finished, have each child use the completed project as a reference to identify the parts of a spider.

Materials for each child:
copy of the spider pattern from the top of page 44
2 pieces of uncooked elbow macaroni
crayons
scissors
glue
four 6" pipe cleaners
8 black hole-punched dots
2' length of white yarn
tape

Steps:
1. Color and cut out the spider pattern.
2. Twist the four pipe cleaners together at the center; then spread them out to resemble eight spider legs.
3. Turn the spider pattern facedown and glue the middle of the twisted pipe cleaners to the lower cephalothorax as shown.
4. Glue the elbow macaroni to the underside of the cephalothorax, as shown, to represent fangs. Allow time for the glue to dry.
5. Set the spider pattern on its legs; then glue the hole-punched dots to the head to represent eyes.
6. Tape one end of the white yarn to the underside of the spider pattern to represent a dragline.

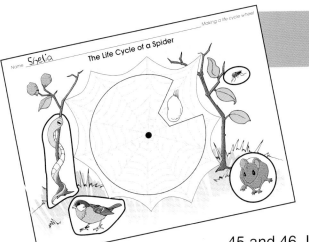

Spider Life Cycle
(Making a Life Cycle Wheel)

Get a leg up on the life cycle of a spider with this clever web wheel! To prepare, make a class supply of pages 45 and 46 and gather a class supply of brads. Begin the activity by explaining that baby spiders, or spiderlings, begin their lives as eggs inside an egg sac. Further explain that soon after the spiderlings hatch, they leave to find a new home, grow into adults, and have baby spiders of their own. Then have each child color a copy of pages 45 and 46. Instruct the child to cut out the top web and animal patterns on page 46. Then have her stack the top web onto the bottom web on page 45 and insert a brad through the center of both webs. Finally, instruct the child to glue the animal pictures in the appropriate spaces as shown. Have each youngster turn the wheel clockwise to view the life cycle of a spider. Then discuss the spider's enemies and potential prey shown around the web. That's life!

Oh, What a Tangled Web We Weave!
(Recognizing Spiderweb Variety, Art)

Materials for each child:
7" x 7" piece of aluminum foil
eight 1' lengths of white yarn
liquid starch in a shallow pan
sheet of white construction paper
black stamp pad
black marker
scissors
glue
sheet of black construction paper
white crayon

Spiderwebs come in all shapes and sizes! Introduce youngsters to the most common variety of spiderweb with some starchy art! In advance, gather the supplies listed at the right. To begin the activity, explain that some spiders use their silk to make webs. Webs can be shaped like orbs, funnels, or even trampolines! (See the book list on page 40 for books with spiderweb photographs and illustrations to share with students.) Further explain that the most common variety of web is a jumble of threads called a tangled web. Next, guide each child through the steps below to create a tangled web. When the webs are finished, display them on a bulletin board with the title "Oh, What a Tangled Web We Weave!"

Steps:
1. Dip a length of yarn into the liquid starch and place it onto the square of aluminum foil. Repeat the procedure with the remaining yarn, overlapping the yarn to represent a tangled web.
2. Allow at least 24 hours to dry; then remove the web from the aluminum foil.
3. Press a finger on the black stamp pad and then make two fingerprints on the white construction paper to represent the two sections of a spider's body.
4. Use the black marker to draw eight legs and six or eight eyes on the spider.
5. Cut out the spider and glue it to the web.
6. Glue the web to the piece of black construction paper.
7. Write your name on the black paper with a white crayon.

Good Vibrations!
(Simulation)

Did you know that spiders usually have eight eyes, but many have very poor eyesight? Complete this experiment to help youngsters experience how these poor-sighted creatures find their food. To begin, explain to students that a spider cannot see an insect caught in its web, but it can feel the web vibrate as the insect moves. Divide the class into pairs. Give each twosome a three-foot length of string and instruct the students in each pair to stand opposite each other, stretching the string tightly between them as shown. Direct each child to pluck the string and observe the vibrations. Next, have one student in each pair close his eyes while the other student plucks the string. Then instruct the students to switch roles. Afterward, discuss with students how their moving hands vibrated the strings much like a moving insect vibrates a spider's web.

Hunting for Food
(Making a Model)

Did you know that some spiders do not spin webs? Use this model of a trap-door spider to introduce your students to spiders that hunt for their food. In advance, gather the materials listed below. Begin the activity by explaining that hunting spiders rely on speed, strength, and surprise to capture their prey. The trap-door spider is a hunting spider that creates a lid for its burrow out of silk, saliva, and dirt. Further explain that the trap-door spider hides under the lid until an insect walks by. Then it pounces on the insect and drags it down into its burrow. Next, distribute the materials below and guide each child through the steps to make his own model of a trap-door spider. Gotcha!

Materials for each child:

12 oz. foam cup	tongue depressor
glue	tape
sand	scissors
2½" x 4½" tagboard	crayons

brown poster board circle, slightly larger than the cup opening
copy of the spider pattern from the bottom of page 44

Steps:
1. Spread glue on the poster board circle; then sprinkle sand over the glue. Set aside to dry.
2. Color and cut out the spider pattern; then glue the spider to the tagboard for durability.
3. Trim away excess tagboard.
4. Fold the spider on the dotted line; then tape the bottom of the spider to the end of the tongue depressor.
5. Cut a small slit in the bottom of the cup.
6. Slide the tongue depressor into the slit so that the spider is hidden inside the cup.
7. Use one piece of tape to fasten the edge of the poster board circle to the rim of the cup to represent a trapdoor.
8. Push up on the tongue depressor to make the trap-door spider sneak through the trapdoor to capture its prey!

Sticky Web Strands
(Simulation)

Students get into a sticky situation when they discover why insects get caught in a web but spiders don't! To prepare, make a class supply of page 47 and gather a supply of transparent double-sided tape, cotton swabs, and cooking oil. Explain that spiderwebs have both dry and sticky strands of silk. Insects get caught and tangled in the sticky strands. Further explain that spiders don't stick to their own webs because they walk on the dry strands and make a special oil for their feet.

Now make sticky spiderwebs with your youngsters. Instruct each student to color a copy of page 47 and then cut out the insects at the bottom of the page. Next, give each child two seven-inch strips of double-sided tape and have him place the strips on the dotted web lines. Have the student place the insect cutouts on the tape to show how sticky web strands will capture an insect. Then have him point out where the spider could walk without getting stuck. Next, give each child a cotton swab to represent insect feet and have him rub one end along the tape. Discuss the results. Then instruct the child to dip the other end of the swab into the oil. Have him rub the oily swab on the tape to show how a spider's oily feet do not stick to the web. Discuss and compare the results. Have each child place his paper in a resealable plastic bag and take it home to share with family and friends.

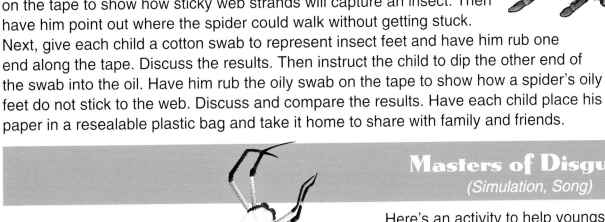

Name Sheldon
No-Stick Spiders!   Simulation

Masters of Disguise!
(Simulation, Song)

Here's an activity to help youngsters understand the benefits of blending in! To begin, give each child a copy of page 48. Instruct her to follow the directions to color the page. Help her cut out the spiders and then tape each one to an ice pop stick to create puppets. Next, sing "Camouflage Song" at the left and instruct each child to place the puppets on the picture according to the verses. When finished, discuss why the spiders in the song cannot be seen by their prey and enemies. Must be camouflage!

Camouflage Song
(sung to the tune of "If You're Happy and You Know It")

I'm a brown and tiny spider, wild and free! Shh! Shh!
I'm not worried; that big bird cannot see me. Shh! Shh!
Oh, that bird cannot see me;
On this fence I'll wait and see.
I'm a brown and tiny spider, wild and free! Shh! Shh!

I'm a green and tiny spider, wild and free! Shh! Shh!
I'm not worried; that big snake cannot see me. Shh! Shh!
Oh, the grass is cool and green
Where I hide and can't be seen.
I'm a green and tiny spider, wild and free! Shh! Shh!

I'm a pink and tiny spider, wild and free! Shh! Shh!
I am hungry, and that bug cannot see me! Shh! Shh!
With a leap and then a crunch,
I can have a tasty lunch.
I'm a pink and tiny spider, wild and free! Shh! Shh!

Name Theresa   Simulation song
Spider Camouflage
Color the ___ brown.
Color the ___ pink.
Color the ___ green.

brown
pink
green

Spider Patterns

Use with "Amazing Spider Anatomy" on page 40.

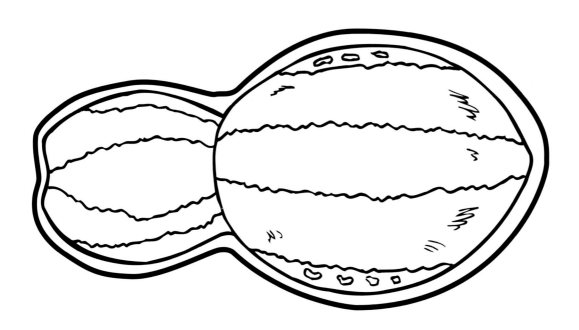

Use with "Hunting for Food" on page 42.

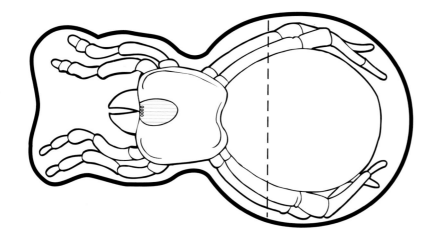

Name _____

The Life Cycle of a Spider

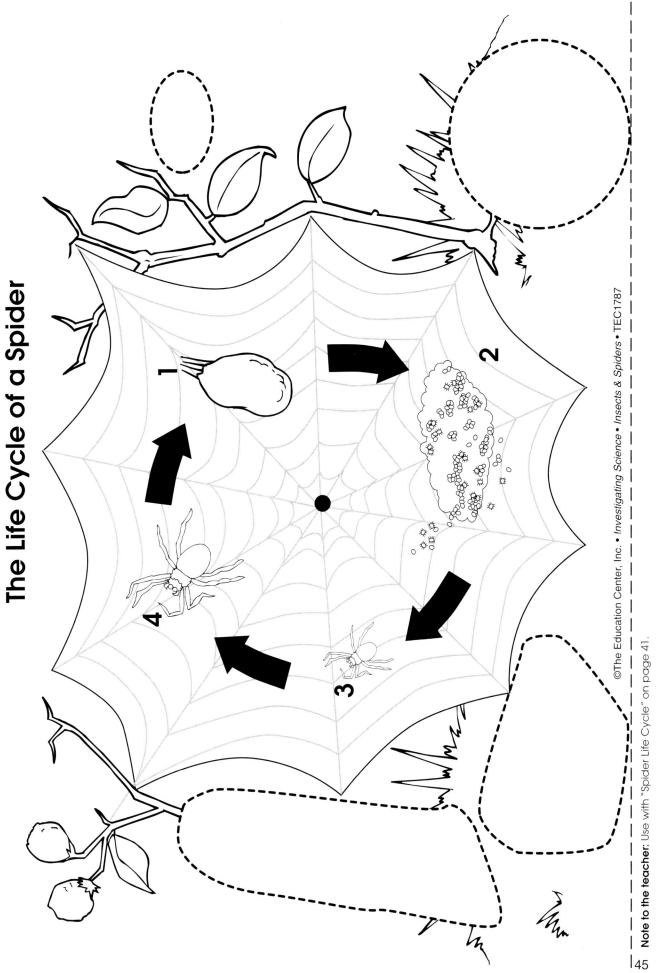

Note to the teacher: Use with "Spider Life Cycle" on page 41.

Web and Animal Patterns

Use with "Spider Life Cycle" on page 41.

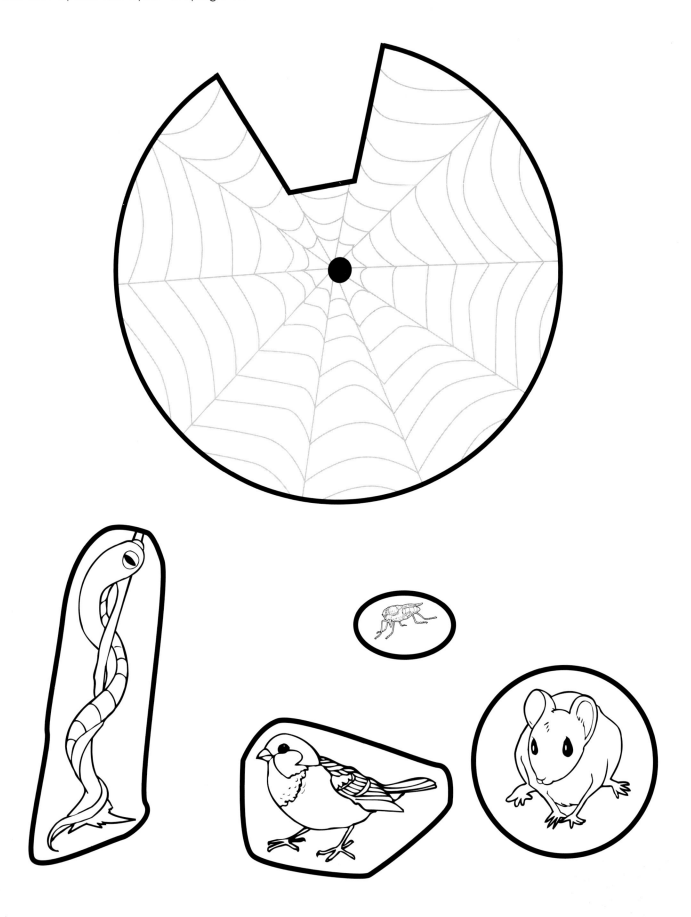

No-Stick Spiders!

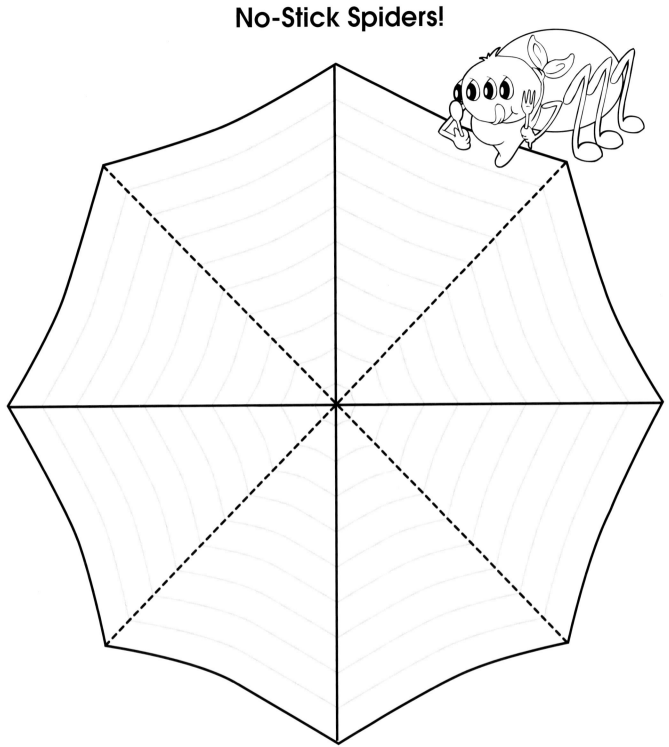

©The Education Center, Inc. • *Investigating Science* • *Insects & Spiders* • TEC1787

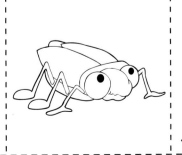

Spider Camouflage

Color the 🖼 brown.
Color the 🖼 pink.
Color the 🖼 green.

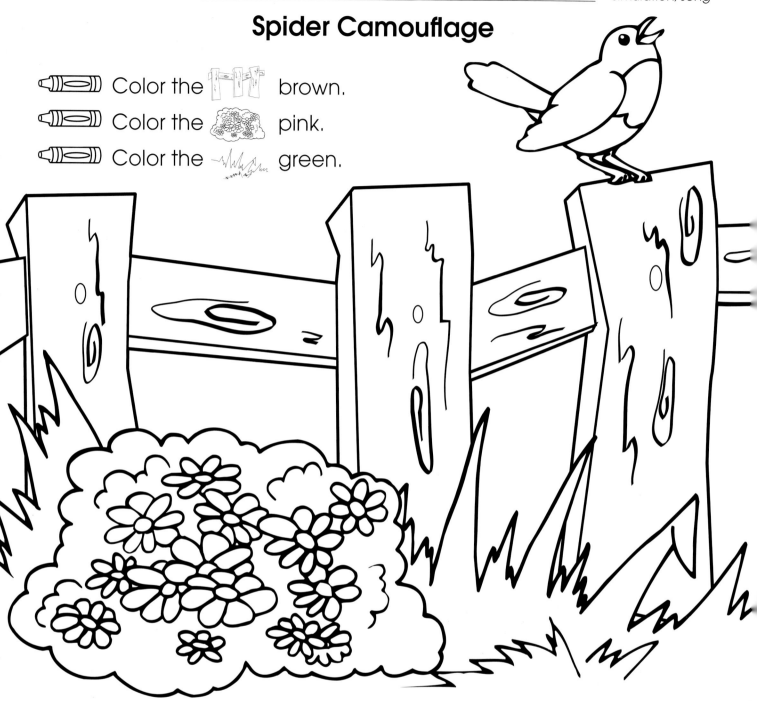

Color the spiders.

brown

pink

green

Note to the teacher: Use with "Masters of Disguise!" on page 43.